Organblooms

¤

Lake Angela

FUTURECYCLE PRESS
www.futurecycle.org

Cover art, mixed media composition with colored pencil cockroach and blooms by Lake Angela and tubercular uterus illustration from Diseases of Women: A Clinical Guide to Their Diagnosis and Treatment *by George Ernest Herman; author photo by Dawn Marie Parker; cover and interior book design by Diane Kistner; Georgia text and American Typewriter titling*

Library of Congress Control Number: 2019949744

Published by FutureCycle Press
Athens, Georgia, USA

ISBN 978-1-942371-80-9

To Delmer Ramers, with gratitude,
and to Kevin Richard Kaiser, with golden birds.

Contents

Part I
PROPHECY

Today...11

Early Memory of Hearing Colors,
 Holding a Cockroach...12

Jesus' Ribs..13

The Hornets..14

Prophet...15

The Wind Dies Last..16

On Watching Helplessly From Your Sickbed
 As the Doctor Takes the Time..............................17

The Deer...18

Psychological Test..20

Things That Are Still Alive...22

Haggling Over the Abyss..23

Love Poem..24

Toward Sleep..25

A Foreign Hotel..26

Human People...27

A Fraction of February..28

Late February..29

What It Would Take...30

Stranded (A Love Poem)...31

Careful Asymmetry...32

Waiting for Spring..33

All We Want..34

Purification...35

A Vision..36

Old Magic...37

God Also Moans..38

This Is the Eye of Time...39

When It Is Time..40

In the Graveyard, Among Stones.....................................41

Love Poem..42

Finding My Way..43

Even So, I'd Like Flowers..44

Dear Master of Colors..45

Points...46

Summer Rain..47

Grandma Sings the Last Song...48

Surrender..49

The Fireworks in the End...50

Part II

LOVE POEM

I Am the Breath That Chisels the Stone.......................................55

Love Poem..56

Love Poem..57

Love Poem..58

Love Poem With Words...59

With a Brief Hour..60

He Demanded Hotter Stars...61

Splitting...62

The Tiny Worlds..63

With the World At War (A Love Poem)...64

Love Over Rain..65

Beauty Tree..66

Love Poem..67

Short Sight...68

Love Poem..69

Love Poem..70

Love Poem..71

Love for God...72

Love Poem..73

Love Poem..74

Grandmother's Love Poem..75

Love Poem..76

Love Poem..77

Love for the Sad Old One..78

Saint's Love Poem...79

The Rules of the Dream..80

Fragments of Love Poems...82

Love Poem..84

Love Poem..85

Love Poem..86

I Return to Find Layers of Dust

    Over the Dream...87

Love Poem..88

Love Poem..89

Part I
PROPHECY

Today

It took all day to bake a cake. I, a prophet or a pagan, stand layered in whipped cream, chocolate under the nails. Kiss me while I cry. Kiss me while I cry. I go somewhere secret to try being alone for real. Where is the blanket? To kiss someone, really kiss, is to let the spirits decide between both sets of lips. "All your friends are ghosts." Except Leonard: Leonard was perfect and responsible. Like a hero, on a walk. How did it happen, that I am living this life? I've noticed how it hurts people.

A tree has been planted inside me. It will throw shadows over me. We come alone and distrustful. Color is our only gift. Yet there is always white noise. No one is calling me. I scribble on paper and wait for the old to take me in, though I still smell my childhood. Take this green and hold it for me. Sometimes, I forget I have skin until somebody touches it.

Early Memory of Hearing Colors,
Holding a Cockroach

I was warned about madness as an infant,
had it from the mouths of demons themselves:
green tongues flicked up the bars that caged
me, unnatural, like neon fire. I recognized the strange
power before I could speak; I understood their language.

My world spun black and white clowns above
me; tiny, misshapen mirrors spread the green glimmers,
all the jack-in-the-box energy about to pop at any moment.

Climb from your crib into a different world—get out,
we'll help, we know the way. You crave brightness; we can give you
more green light. We will always, always be here,
now as a whisper, now a rush of wind

that dies. And rises nearer. Until one day the sulfur damp breath
on my neck never leaves: I want to go back now and shake that infant
myself—tell her take the advice, get out, get out—kill her myself.
Save her, myself.

But that baby in my memory singing such starry sound things to herself,
stroking the armored insect in one hand like a loved one: she doesn't fear
that fear. The world's hurt is still outside her. Her parents come and go,
oblivious, and she smiles and notices everything.
And how can I blame her, really? When the jack has yet to spring
the box, when I still walk through the green cast shadows, trusting it all?

Jesus' Ribs

As a child I looked at Jesus on the cross and noticed
his ribs, each well formed and sticking out at me like pointing fingers.

Long and sickly, the ribs summoned me, bending to the point
of breaking like tree branches as they motioned, *come closer,*

but they never broke. The branches twisted round my heart,
crushing and squeezing bits of crimson. He had so much power

over me, a death grip. I couldn't look away. *Keep me alive,*
he whispered. *Keep me alive...*I saw his holy mouth move.

I was four years old and feared Sundays with him talking to me
while hanging from the ceiling, dangling over the black figure

of the priest. It was then I decided I wanted to be thin. I wanted
to look at my chest and see the tree branches in the ribbed arch

where Jesus held tight to my heart.

The Hornets

The once-swarming hornets are now in hiding,
the hive another ghost town. They are easy
to know, if anyone would only take the time.
When I was a child I hid in closets to see
how long it took for someone to miss me.
The hornets, the hide and seek, are not meant
to be dangerous. The buzzing you shrink
from is only a warning—it is easily solved.
Hornets are carriers of a wandering death,
and the child scoops them into the empty jar
whose bright berry stains she can faintly smell,
with a taste she can almost remember. She shuts
the lid on the hornets, places them in the closet,
not wishing to hide the black bullets that pang
the glass panes with whole bodies, but for you.
She does this so you don't have to hear them;
what she does not smell, taste, feel you are years
nearer to finding. The hornets know what they must
do: act angry; tear furious, winged holes through
this coast and the next; be heard, not seen.
Spread the word.

Prophet

Some wind is caught in the thorn
bushes. A sun shadow glows red.
It is midday when trumpets sound
and announce sunrise—no one
apologizes for the delay. The ants
have hurried into their diminutive
pyramids; the strong oaks listen
to the shades of silence, nearly
afraid to breathe. No rodent stirs
behind his walls. A bat slaps an oak
and, in the shock, neither squeals.
What is happening here? The late
sun looks like dust. A policeman
rushes to fetch the madwoman
from her restraints, but she is gone
and the book of dreams all ablaze.
The man wants to weep; where
do we go from here?

The Wind Dies Last

This hot yellow day dawned centuries ago
and now the air is stale. At first the anger
storm was a shock; now it spins like a dusty
angel caught in a cycle of weary memories,
among them snow. All the children are old.
The circus was to come but lost the way,
and meantime the flies wandered off
on their own: confusion is unbearable.
Where will they go in the cold? None of us
knows because summer has been here so long.
Eventually the wind must rise to breathe
a eulogy: everyone listens for the sound
of weeping reeds. Who will give the wind's
eulogy? It is hard, we have found, to bury
something unblack or become nothing. Burial
occurs in a darkness sealed by centuries,
but in this fearless daylight nothing moves.

On Watching Helplessly From Your Sickbed
As the Doctor Takes the Time

Content with your payment,
the witch doctor—
who you know is a healer
because you trust your schizophrenia
to recognize another two-spirited woman
—packs her sand.
Before she leaves,
she tips the voyeur clock's
face from the wall
into her sack, tacks
your crumpled old paper bag
in its place.
And though you know
you must watch the bag
at the prescribed times,
you will never understand,
even with your wide eyes
and sleepless attention to fearfulness,
now that the clock is gone.

The Deer

He told me what he rode here was a deer,
how gracefully her back bent
for him, how her pink tongue lapped the rain
when he wouldn't let her stop,
not even in late summer when the voices
of the reservoirs were silenced by green decay.

He said he shot the doe to watch her decay—
that's why I couldn't ride the deer.
He held his body erect, but the dead's voices
I think tormented him, the way he bent
his neck too far back and didn't stop
blinking into the sky, pretending it was because of the rain.

He said it was he who slaughtered the rain
and let it fall over the late summer decay.
He said he possessed the power to stop
God in the woods, tired God limping toward the deer;
and gun down God, too, until He bent
over His crumpled creation, until guilt-ridden voices

screeched, until he extinguished the voices
of burning angels, on their white stars, with the cold rain
that slants over fields where bent
bodies struggle like fish and their quick decay
rambles over the burnt-gold field, the tarnished deer
soggy with bloated summer's death, a death that will not stop.

There is no power, he thinks, great enough to stop
him crushing my bones in his teeth, licking severed voices
from his lips. Unexpected children with deer
innocence laugh from a hidden cave—or is it rain
falling in bullets that thump the decay
of beasts as though it were possible to kill one body twice? He's bent

on overthrowing God so that the deity is bent
on His knees, His last breath suspended like a prayer that won't stop,
a breath that reeks like late apple rot and sweet grass decay,
a smoldering garbage graveyard condemning the voices
of the laughing children to lives of empty rain.
He has erected a shrine with the dead deer
around him, droning with bent and rusted voices
that anger him, and he brims madness because he can't stop the rain,
and his savage teeth decay like yellow lace, useless, because for all his
effort he is unable to swallow the spirit of the deer.

Psychological Test

Her voice can make flowers grow— Evil spirits possess me— Stars
are sharded glass for our good. Perpetual street-light people fooled
into staggering out in darkness— Frequently, I am called by my number.
Chronological time supposed to comfort, warn the night of the origin
of sadness. Is it important to think, act, then feel? My soul atrophies:
I am addicted— Most people are sick in some way. The only cure
for the Middle Ages was wormwood, poppy for the pain. Crazy
Horse— More than one voice— What the sun needs— When it is thought
I cannot hear, I am called number 16. Possible to drug angels—also
walk in human skins. Roaches shall inherit earth.

In death, all eyes are blue, the spirit composed of two only. There goes
the old tree, climbing up again— The most frightening thing, the non-
color— Hard to escape the skin— To try and remember is scary because
I may not— When I was excited to sleep for the next dream—against age
— They are said to have been blessed with good waters. The stars
translate God for us, while the soul strains along on hands and knees—
Always the most functional or the most beautiful— The eye of everything
— The calmest place: the graveyard, the library. Why do you come
and go, my dear?

The smile expresses endurance and determination— The tigers behind
bars see double— Longing to breathe— Most people have trouble
breathing regularly— Does your skin become sand on the beach? There is
too much at stake: as much a problem as the problem is— I found a little
laughter buried alive in the war—

To trust wholly in sleep is why I must not. What else has He ever been?
A man walks in wearing underfed clowns and no eyes: remember,
I have hidden my nightmares under the bed since childhood— It is
indecent to be sick in a painting. I knew a woman once who gave me
this body— On the carousel, sharks replaced the glittered ponies—
Dandelions, sunflowers' ancestors— We do our best work in bed.
Smell that rain? What did God put in that rain? Hope for the chickens—
I prefer synesthesia to art. Only way to remember: burn his name
with light— And to make a better person, paint a halo around it.

I am home: a village in animal skin and cruelty. Blue eyes portend
blindness— The air smells of prisons and blonde hair woven
with buttercups— We are still looking for the secret room— If anyone
could, the house cat— They say we dream, but we only sleepwalk
to the sounds of hollowed memories. The upside of being beaten
is ideas are shaken loose— I wish there was a basket
I could carry myself in.

Things That Are Still Alive

The clock sits in the cage with panther, tapping
arthritic fingers. The panther paces to the jerking beat.
We wait for a sword of sun to slash the bars.
In the children's petting zoo, a small garden of brains
waves glowing stems at the dark.

The living sleep in the graveyard and wake
already dressed in bridal gowns spun by their dead
while the sleepers gave rise to slow breaths.

The artist can count his days by the tree stumps in his pupils.
God closes his eyes and lets his hands
handle the creating. He prefers to kneel
like a child in his gardens. He prefers his castle
in ruins. God is just
romantic that way.

Haggling Over the Abyss

You, looking for refuge: as a runaway myself,
wandering in glass forests, eventually I broke
into light. I bought a bag of sugar and a sack
of love for a bargain price. The traders here
say there is a place underwater where the wind
and rain won't touch. The light must strain.
It is hard to hear one's voice, to breathe even,
to concentrate on the dark ones who invade
and refuse to leave. I think you may find it
quite safe here.

Love Poem

The night rode in; it came
to you, fawn, the wise.
No more errors: it slit
straight through you; it slid
down a dark chamber in your heart.
It hurt you.

Toward Sleep

Angels moan under the weight
of wet wings; they dip low over the Lake.
Organ groans strain to mask sounds
of the struggle. The strong yellow beam
from the lighthouse snuffs out;
a silver hand slips over my mouth.
The wind is gone. I won't fall to sleep.

A Foreign Hotel

I woke up in a strange, slanted room.
Pigeons wept and rocked on the window sill;
I wasn't sure what the problem was.
Gargoyles kept their eyes fixed on the roof
while pigeons smeared them with excrement.
The windows were open in between
iron bars. With one hand outside,
I could feel cool rain. I touched some drops
to my lips; they were bitter. I gagged.
Downstairs, the walls were raw stone.
The concierge was an austere figure
who said I had not checked into this hotel—
he expressed no puzzlement—nevertheless,
I could not leave. *You can't be serious,*
I thought. *How did this happen to me?*
You had choices, he said.

Human People

In a skull a fire burns.
Many people camp around.
They pray, folded into each other.
Eye sockets bleed dim yellows.
Those who take refuge here find
themselves mute. They pound
on the skull walls with a few dull
stones, with fewer withered ideas.
They hope shamelessly.
One woman or man scratches
into the gray tissue what looks
to be an oversized eye or a sun:
He will see us home.
But the fire rises; no stars come;
outside there is no wind.
Inside the lovers curled into
each other no longer stir. The rest-
less clap their tools. A stone falls
into the fire, a hollow sound
that seems like, *Listen;*
we are nearly out of light.

A Fraction of February

Shut your ears to the screams
of souls in labor. Shriek a bird
chirp nest of empty eggs, mess
of dead animals scattered around.
Keeper gutted a woman today—
to remove the child. It was necessary.
Keep away from the maddened
old woman who guards the ground
where carnage remains. Stay away.
Who will sweep up? The usual
custodian is not paid enough.

Late February

Welcome to the show. My show.
I wear a bird in my hair. Its teeth
fall out—that's the point, too tiny
to notice.

What It Would Take

My womb, if it exists, is not a starry
underwater dark to harbor a beginning
life. Inside is a desert where wrinkled
mad ones crouch at the ends

of their days, waiting to swallow one
mouthful of God. There is no kindness in me
for the perfectly helpless. There is no country
in this world that can nurture that innocence.

I am a hard devotee, an expanding
desert, a fractured planet cracking off
in every direction in search of the Infinite.
And I have not seen the kind of love it would take.

Stranded (A Love Poem)

Before I let love graze my skin, no matter how much I ache,
I ask a critical question, a test in which I am the dangling
worm, the living bait. I wonder, *If we were stranded*
on a sun-scorched island, with nothing to consume but sparse
grass blades and morning dewdrops, tell me—would you
eat me? That way one of us might still be saved, and I want
to be the saving muscle: take this body, sink your teeth in,
the way you did as a child licking from the red pools over
ridges of collarbone. Drink slowly. Lick your lips redder.
Sharpen your teeth on clean-picked bone. Chew every bit
with care—let me see you savor each piece of me as no
one has before you, and no one else ever will—until
my eyes fade, my skin-glow snuffs out. Then weep for
life's success, the empty beauty, the stripped carcass.
In fact, promise me you'll do it, my brother: eat me in the end
if it looks like I am coming to nothing; and, while you do,
you can describe to me the ways in which each part is beautiful.
I want to be eaten, and you, who understands me without words,
have promised to walk with my skins wrapped tight around you.

Careful Asymmetry

There are hawks in the half tree, black
and still as child-sized coffins.
They are seven and loom above
gleaming wet grass with its freckles
of violet flowers; and, after, the abyss:
cliffs, nothing for a fall, then Lake.

Hawks rise above all, wings serrated
like a shawl made of knives when they spread
and slice through sky, sprinkling bits of blue
into the Lake. Who are they coming to carry away?
The tree with branches on only one side portends:
laked roots stirring something through the deep.

Waiting for Spring

Behind their fogged window panes, priests drape cool cassocks on;
they long to disappear from December. They will stay this way
all winter. The meadowlark hides in my head. Careful, white rabbit:
the foxes are out. Oblivious and intrepid creatures who offer
running prayers stay safe. The snow is so high the children must tunnel
out—its oil-black underbelly seems to have a heartbeat. Sure enough,
the prophet who turns the clock hands in God's absence foreshadows
a pair of lovers entwined in white-limbed bareness with terrible
smiles still stiff on their faces when the snow thaws. When magic recedes
and the new world becomes the old again, the priests creep out
silently, still draped in brown. The insects peer from holes; the children
blink, their endless tunnel is gone, and they awaken to find they are old
already. When the world turns halfway, the sun, set free, signals us:
the priests raise their brown arms; the aged children open ancient
mouths and croak the song of the sun. The insects chirp. Soon the birds
will return home, the yellow ones last of all. Then priests will shed
shadows and long robes and step up to the altar: the earth is soft
enough; the world is ready now to bury the loosening dead.

All We Want

These things we hold together
shriek in our hands:
like the like sides of magnets,
they can't stand to touch.

We rock against
a world-weight stone;
God's hands—the left,
the right—have never formally met.

Imagine: in another lifetime,
this man could give birth.

Purification

A wind with fangs, the flowering
blessed lungs, a fistful of magic
bursting into bloom. A winter creation,
so crystalline in its absolute cold,
it's off-limits to the ugly.
The shape of a woman that rose
in place of the moon—at last,
a blue breath—has hovered
for months. In her black shadow
one finger of light grazes lips—
shhh—and flicks out; the night
is cooling into wonder, becoming
nameless, losing its created shape.

A Vision

And I saw the end
of dreams.
A vast rolling hill
called heaven,
with grass green as eyes
that the sun, eye of the world,
commands. And I saw
a candle made of waxed moon,
the land for dreams ignited;
the birds all swayed around the ring,
for there are in every world
those things that can fly,
those beings with wings.
The death angel danced with flame,
swaying black and shimmering as diamond-
dark ice. These are expensive
sacrifices: time, blood, life,
the dreams the angel wished out,
the sun waiting with eyes clenched closed,
still in morning.

Old Magic

Old Magic Woman whittled
to seamless soul, lies shining glass,
at water's edge
an unworn cold.
This is the Lake she loves.

But the sailors' hands dipped in blue,
dipped deep in amber, bottle greens,
weather. The gulls' beaks slice thin—
and thinner beneath the sky's thin:
they turn the sky sunset.

And the fish
hook their gaping jaws and turn
their eyes away—away, because they cannot
close them. They don't want to tell;
the Lake whispers to the children
and there are no
secrets from the cold.

The Great Lake rattles, taunts
a rim of light around
blue ridges. She has no
eyes of her own. Irises dry
along the bank; people plod over
black, magic disks sunk in sand
where heavens blink
behind misplaced pupils. The children
collect the wilting eyes, weigh the worlds in their hands:
vision thrusts at them;
but they remember their plastic colored pails,
toss their eyes in.

God Also Moans

Hear that? Do you hear?
The moaning train, the painful
Lake calling for her eyes;

the lighthouse hit
by thunder. The Lake drums. One more
angel drowns in murky water.

This Is the Eye of Time

It blinks steel hail,
seven colors of earth;
its lid washed with fire,
the tears steam.

A blind star flees
the splintering eye:
it will grow warmer in the world
and the dead will be nearer
to blooming.

When It Is Time

The body is made for a movement
it has yet to catch up to. Dull my fingertips
and still they can't handle fire. The roads
are paved over and my feet are torn.
In all this gray, I don't know whether to turn
back, to stoop or crawl, or which way is forward.
I am told that if a shark stops to sleep,
she dies; when the sun sleeps the world
is powered by dreams. This creature dreams a god.
We walk until our bodies are worn and we turn
gray; our hearts have strong calluses,
and we are tired from dreams that happen
only while we sleep, of feeling for the lights
with burnt fingertips only to find damp stone
and more darkness. Gravestones erode
to namelessness because it no longer matters
what each was called. Even stone gray
will erode one day and the smattering of beings left
behind will warm themselves by the fire—
the first and darkest light. In the open
air, they will breathe the silence and grow
strong. Soon it is time to die.

In the Graveyard, Among Stones

Open-armed I stand—feet freezing to earth, windblown
blonde hair darkened for the occasion—into wildness.
Into the cemetery. People used to picnic here more often.
I see very few strangers anymore, though their dead
are all around. This age is the middle of love. *Come
as you are to me,* the stones crack like God's icy voice.
Here among the headstones we open our minds and trade
them. The angels are weightless but must carry the bulk
of the world. I never have been a tree—how could I?—
so strong, so stable. The silence of my Lake is long.
I'd like to be lost in a forest with you who show me
luminous things so simply, with feelings we think wise
and unbeatable. I wouldn't mind drowning in your eyes.
You reach for me and my skin blooms. I long for a longer
touch, my heartbeat breaking up with age like a creaking
glacier, melting snow into your cupped palms. This age
is brutal: we are in between; dreams run through us
like water, but we thirst. My veins itch and my skin
that bursts into bloom, fiercely for you,
will wither soon.

Love Poem

I hold a white
tree, the hip bone
bare as teeth
we touch.

Finding My Way

I pick flowers in the yellow meadow of somebody else's story,
run down the old cobblestone hill in a fleecing rain, the dew leftovers
dull from last night's drunken stars. Lit streetlamps catch the rain
in an act no one wants to stop, the crime is so breathtaking.

Far away, behind many walls, he draws a steaming bath or stands,
perhaps, at the mirror to shave. I shiver on the hill, slip on wet stones
through a past I cannot hold, even in the grip of a young memory.
This cannot be my story.

I pick poppies that match the welts on my body, tongue the dew
without relief. I gather streaks of color that grow familiar: arrange bright,
bruised petals into a quiet bouquet of memories to present to him
when I find my way back.

But the thin lives wilt as I wait before a locked door for someone
to come, from any direction.

Even So, I'd Like Flowers

I would never say it aloud, but
I want you to give me a disheveled
flower, one that falls to pieces,
drastically, at your feet. Gold-crowned,
shivering in its own light, not knowing
light is warmth. I, who oppose
choking the flower from its stem
for show, for a lover's smile; murdering
or breeding refrigerated reds
that never did nor will smell like roses
or anything but cold—yes, I would
like one from you. A sunflower, or even
a lighted smile, or anything wrapped
in tissue paper and surrounded
by clinging baby's breath worshipping:
my own torn organs on a stem.

Dear Master of Colors

Glass clouds catch
on a ledge of stone sky.

I don't oppose loss as long as
someone is looking at us.

Filth and black stars.
And the sign we mistook for surrender.

Points

What will you scribe on my tombstone,
doctors? Will you be the ones to write
with milk-glove hands? Will you,
businessmen, be responsible for this
love, prune her, sing to her? The world
is my love's grave, just as the Lake
is her own grave. The dead are buried
facing East, but the stars—ah, the stars
bow their eyes and lay down their lives.
O, to weep from every point. The last
goes up in flaming tears. Blackened
princes clap an encore in champagne.

Summer Rain

And it will last all night:
sit in the full bathtub
on Grandma's front porch
that crumbles in the rainlight.
Cold rain pours with abandon,
and your body warms the streams
that slap your skin. A cicada is brave,
or is it the porch swing that creaks
under weary God's weight?
Strangers come alone are welcome
to wash in the Old Magic
Lake, everything water:
black sky and wandering
pink moon, with the sailors
lost in it.

Grandma Sings the Last Song

She looks at the Lake
and sees her god dancing
on top. Grandma blesses
herself and feeds the Old
Magic some bright glass,
green bottles.

The Lake warns: in ten years,
Grandma's cliff will crumble; water
is only something for sky to float on
and dream.

Grandma goes home to make
an offering of her house; she begins
to invite the gulls for supper.
She sits at the piano and plunks
the keys in water.

They drift off on blues,
music between the teeth.
When Old Magic Woman sings,
her voice spills into ripples.

Sit on the bank, wrap yourself
in clouds: grandchild, watch
the sound turn colors.

Surrender

Old Magic Woman bent at the shore
sifts through glass on her knees,
listens for bells from the distant sea,
keeps watch from Lake's edge—
exiled.

She strains through her cataracts
like a grandmother, but deadly,
signals for secret medicine—
wrings the silent, salt-puffed clouds
that shake a reluctant bit of water loose.
But a drop is not enough.

A steel-blue window, intact,
washes up on timid waves.
Something is ending,
rattle the chilly gray fish.

The gulls turned gray watch behind
spindled wings: the proud old woman lifts
her battered magic hands high,
takes off her ancient face.

The Fireworks in the End

Inclined late over the ocean, among the choking
reeds, all the stars are busy drowning. A brazen
soldier once talked of crossing the sun. When he
died, of course, in the end it was tuberculosis.

Run to the shadow with me—hurry: fire reigns
in your blue forest and your mouth wide with awe.
Your kisses have rusted; nothing with wings lasts.
I like when you say you crossed the ocean to visit

my heels. I hear gravestones are a bargain now.
How would you feel about being buried together?
Those beautiful things, skies full of wings and blue
eyes that blink too fast for us, carry the plague

to our doorsteps: a love gift, a dead rat I lifted
a hundred times with bare hands. Look over this
horizon; tell me what you see. Is it time to say
I love you? I cannot handle seeing the carps'

eerie heads, hammer eyes. The sun and darkness merge
and grow obese black fruits. Those who can't reach
must wait. One plunges but snags a single twilit strand
and dangles.

The ocean is nearly over; the waves lose the time
to soothe our feet. Come, call the bulging beast with me.
Love demands it: beast with muted words, opened
mouth, spitting hatred and spinning sadness into sweet

poison. I understand God has lost his mother.
As birds migrate to another realm, we follow the fish
gleaned to bone, gulp pieces of bread, make wishes
and blow out our lives. We miss the fireworks

in the end, the ship that sails sleeping passengers
returning globed souls to the sunset. We stretch
our years apart. I will see you in another lifeboat,
I say. No patience in this world could keep us safe.
Or perhaps we will never meet.

Part II
LOVE POEM

I Am the Breath That Chisels the Stone

The pigeon peaks, and a minor confusion ripples
through his wings in flight.

The nun fills the dry night with her streaming
feeling, noticing the stars are not enough.

You: song, war: bring the stone to your lips
and become his, her mouth so stone can speak.

The boy only knew green fruits flung
midday, by the hundreds, from the tallest trees.

Creation's mother is nearby: the break of day,
flowers in a vase, the sponge, the spilled wine,

her tenderness to touch. Be still. You control
energy and the flow of names from your mouth.

Sweet mouth, soft lips; the thunderous beauty
of the minute breath nears.

Love Poem

for Leonard

My childhood is mostly shadows: your gray suit,
your woolen eyes. Your love deep, green, pervasive.
You made me your river; you made me your glove.
Now the other hand is bare, not cold. You are strong
although very old, although I have never seen you
make a fist—save once to crush the glass that spread
the wine of my red birth.

Love Poem

I have heard that I should disappear.
The voices say.
A ring holds me up. I balance
on silence that's beautiful:
there is always nothing more to say.
In favor of feeling—
I feel.
Still, a voice tells me
I should disappear
although I have been shot at,
the calling cards of predators tucked
in my pockets.
What is the difference
between girls and boys, they say,
and I can tell you too much.
But I have not remained beautiful enough.

I, you are still hungry, and I know
what your-my stomach craves. I have decided
to let you-me starve now,
so I am no longer afraid. Art is anything
that refuses to die out. The circle, the lemur.

I hated the sea for being so much more.
I was once unafraid and therefore
no longer myself.
For the first time now
I have been myself unafraid.

Who goes hunting for the gazelle? My time.
And once the worms have been summoned
there will be no chance of retreat.
They do not invade, as some say, but suggest.
They are the guests of circumstance—
and fate.

Unkillable and immortal are not the same.

Love Poem

Not this flute-flood! These words need me: these words like stones
still keeping the shore down, though only remnants now. The need
also remains. The trees who took the water in all those years have
grown great, and on each leaf an eye blooms with a word; each
thinks always of its difference and how odd we no longer know
each star by name. The last earthen being to know each one is gone.
There are no months, only moths in the forest of night hungering
for the breach of light we fortunate ones have come to expect.
One day it will be again yesterday, and someone will rise up
in the form of a blue deer and remember how to speak to the trees
and how to listen. Poetry will be discovered newly born and naked
in the thornbush, untorn and already at play with a cool breeze
from behind us. A voice on the breeze calls out to us, too: unpack
our feet so carefully tucked away and stray from the dying gray
spines of sidewalks—back from the yellow room to the broken fields,
ready to re-collect the broken blue days.

Love Poem With Words

My memories have misplaced me and mistaken me
for someone else. I hunt for light in the caves
of every hollow black room. Home gives itself up
in an instant—at once recognizable by its dormant,
ghosting pains. White light before lament, a shield
composed of mirrors lets me pass.

White so that men will speak from holiness, of holiness,
encaged in a forlorn mountain, the range of peaks
a pen for cattle of all colors and nations. It must
get worse; the spice has fallen from a forest once
forbidden—to ghosts. But now your child is back
there with a knife, in your room.

Speak, speak: flight is an idiom of unknowing, unwinding
the long tapes of memory blighted by nightfall
after bruising red night lives—lost torsos, lost planets.
But we've come this far, from stolen place to stolen
place. Perhaps there is something more to tell. How
do you make up for such a long, lost, barren time?

Goodbye, rooms full of beautiful words, glimmering on.
I am not called by any of your names. Your learning
has not yet lifted you from this light-bitten, flea-black
hole. Perhaps audaciously—pardon—I ask one more task
of our long-struggling love to my death: Love,
compose for me your fanfare.

With a Brief Hour

Watch:
unwritten, the sails
with your name in mind
fly out upon the sea, waving hello,
and at once goodbye, without a word.

Join us at noon, swimming light, with a touch.

Wax candles,
wood frames.
With burning rings the lovers stand
together, head upon breast. Molten, the chalice,
the wood structure slouched like a shadow under moon.

Little deer, gone so long
and not returned. Bridal, the hour, so long
the light.

He Demanded Hotter Stars

I locked myself in November, an entire life
quite pale, nearly lightless. To believe
in the art of a cloud. All alone, pulling apart:
to give birth like that, with the southward
screams of birds behind me, the clenched fingers
singeing each other. Holding one's breath
is a museum of speaking also. The words
ice over; water whispers gleam like a vast,
blanched moon bone. My body is this: colorless
spheres, frost-burned fingers, and thoughts
from a world that deals in fleeting heat,
flickering lives. I would not wish on stars
but grow so cold as to sleep with fire.

Splitting

Grandfather, weak fever, color of choking lungs:
I cannot breathe through all this water, my Lake on fire.

Yellow butterflies pin down my arms at the elbows.
Twist the faucet and blue clouds squeeze from metal pores, drift.

In the mirror my face glows yellow; I see
your dead mouth superimposed.

Dark purple calls me closer, curls up to me like a cat.
All along the path rustling bushes break into birds!

My earthbound soul contracts, *relax*. Who knew trees have genders?
Who knows I am the old man around my neck?

She speaks for ghosts. (Why don't the ghosts speak for themselves?)
Rainbow cliffs in the moonstone. I am dripping honey

from my bee's orifice. I am a dead child. Nothing is risen:
rather, blue has descended

to touch with soft teeth our humbly holy feet. Surrender
your teeth, your white fangs, your knife face!

Poor cat, hoping I'll pet him, trailing me, twirling his tail
and talking to birds. Perhaps I have not been enough.

Outside, the pecan tree bursts into song. Scrambled birds watch
with approval, the teachers of song like black leaves slickly shining.

To live and die in a river, a mirror. To be outside myself:
to strike two stars together in chime.

The Tiny Worlds

Does a poem mean nothing to her brother?
Luminous with phlegm and forgotten? The tree of love
casts shade over the aching earth of the dead, honed by the sharp
teeth of diminutive voles, steel files, false nails, and the sickle claws
of all the old spirits. Frustrated night, for peace
is wrung out and abandoned in the brush.

Meanwhile each mouth is a three-cornered anecdote; at least three.
Futures are bought and distributed at every business meeting, every
businessman's gold dream. The massless guffaws of the murderers rise,
hope left in the good hands of industrious nuthouses: the operations
that profit secrets, secreting mouths tongue-tied, newly named
and ready—to issue a line of newer names. Industrious, the dreamless.

A life—each one—an experiment. Already accomplished. Check.

The rats', the mosquitoes' lives, their blood paid in full
in the labs of our owners. The nights, the distinctions, the deciding genes.
The rabbits want revenge before they die in peace, in pieces,
in reverse. This art kills, delivers daily doubt and discomfort,
brands with words in smoke, combinations of letters
that don't make sense except as constellations far removed.
And even then: luminous phlegm, forgotten.

With the World At War (A Love Poem)

Even the poets fight, striking each other with words.

With spirits black as the country night, the lovers court
each other's bandaged hearts.

When we heard we first fashioned for our dreams the gleaming
black boxes once meant for love poems, then buried them,
separately, in the black loam deepest hidden in our bodies.

The same bodies, we discovered, were vast worlds of tangled waters
deep with new dreams glowing soft with sleep on more softly lit ledges.

Discouraged by the breadths of the opposing hands rich
in fingers, we were intimidated by mouths: that the only way in
seemed a black cavern of teeth much too sharp.

And though black birds fly out, no golden bird will carry us in.

The earth is broken, tracks of bone exposed, the lakes salted
with blood; we must discover some other place to ease our thirst.
The sky is the last place:

she, he drifts, colorless, lightless, free for the taking. It is up to us
to reach our hidden burial mounds and unravel the rivers:
we have lost track of our black boxes and given our hearts up.

Alone, I fear for the sky—that even the lovers may try
to conquer him, her—and how easily he will give herself
to the auspices of love.

Love Over Rain

Rain over the masks of the year.
Rain on an absolute, rain dissolving the painting.
Murmurs in the mouths of the gods turn to sleeping
creatures, borne of wet fur and words,
water roses in the colors of eyes.

The rain sings and sings; the impregnated spirit
stirs. She opens her mouth, the spirit,
drinking walls into light and joy into light.

Rain over the paintings, pools of shining colors
across the hours, the many masks, the factory
of silence covered over by more—
rain over the mouth of the year, a drop on a lower lip, lingering.

Beauty Tree

The city's black bones struck by lightning.
Now the skeletal capital of spite stands against
its own cold throbbing throat. From the empty gut
the gazelle rights the wind—against her self-
same soul to stand.

Dying doesn't happen standing down; standing
engenders the Word. Without comprehending,
the ear blind beats the drum made upon a canvas
of star-stretched, wound-deep sky. This way
to comprehension is ending and elastic. It calls
for a re-evolution.

Revolution will come, so enjoy its coming.
Rifle buried in an unmarked site: when the world
continues and warms a little longer—the last
rusted bullet will shoot up through shocked brown
dirt a gold tree, whole and holy. The veins
of her branches will be the origin
of beauty—of many dangerous, new, broken hearts.

Love Poem

Held within its nest of thorns, the newborn
heart must learn to lift its heavy head.
Born blind, it will not develop any sign
of sight, only symbols to hold the place
in a matter of eyes. It will sense so keenly
the deer drinking from the stream below
to know the treacherous twists and turns
of the wandering lifeline—its aim entrenched,
fervent, in heralding flicks of color like wings.
Just steel is foreign; so too are the crutches
we, machining, adhere to. As the second
guess is never as good, rest at first.
The incredible delicate being will understand
in you power.

Short Sight

There will be another eye,
a freed desert full with fog,
the sunburn sucked inward keeping
at last to sun's self, dumb,
having robbed himself of her very mouth.

Come womb, give birth to the stolen
again; let us call new
whatever rises here with a whimper,
a wart and yellow skin like rocks,
underneath which the worms stall
for time, buying the finest of webs
spider abandoned
to mist over ragged cliffs.

Before the child's soft head turns
hard, remember to tell it: stone
and you were sister and brother
once.

Love Poem

You achieved your calluses by holding up trees to brace
the sky in turn. That never kept the gray from descending,
the life of the stone from seeping in—and changing you.

And I rise from luminous seas sopping rich with the residues
of different births.

I am still held up by stitches of God, each one as strong
as it is indispensable. For what should be my new fate
if my web of guilt and the sinews of the blue animal sorrow

should break? I am unborn again and have the impression
that hell smells as benign as chlorine—

relatively! And that a man in a suit with a round starched
collar assembles my body; carefully Father fills each limb
with sawdust until I am not quite awake—but erect.

How much love lavished on the Age of Stone instead?
If love in time, then more than I have ever known.

In light of this knowledge, when you hear next our grandfathers
calling us back, will you be nearer?

Love Poem

Be silent with me as the trees are silent,
knowing every word without name.
In the nightly birth of skies—
insistent, foolish—the ghost takes his meal.
On your face the expression of a hand.

Two great fingers descend through the firmament.
We cannot swear
that they feel anything, that it even happens.
Behind a shudder of clouds they dip down,
perform a murder, and go free.

Nights on earth
in grieving windows, linens hanging over.
The sick homesick in white retreat
after the long hunts for their souls.
Beneath bandages they harbor sores filled with nearness, endless
hurting for wounds with permanence.
The ghost licks deep, drawn by heat.

The murderer halts outside, his hand held high—
the breath of fugitives shines like coins;
the moon squeezes into the door frame unbathed—
let us lie sharply, our branches erect.

Love Poem

The sky has sunk in failure,
and the seeds are hearts wrenched from home
in the furtive pause that precedes the dawn: when all eyes,
like the great black hearts of sunflowers, are turned towards God.

A murder in the wake
of the great yellow tidal wave mesmerizes—
so that even the hummingbird forgets to guard his heart.

Creation is estranged from its organs.
Notes sound from a hollow of a far-off flute.
God's breath grants us our freedom—a solemn word
whose meaning has been given its honorable discharge.

Love for God

Perhaps you can tell me, what does luck
have to do with this divine plan? So far, it seems,
and you have misplaced places. Time
and again you have called me
by the wrong names. Or perhaps
it is I furiously mimicking the words
who does not understand the language;
I who linger in some stranger's house drinking
the tea with no name, the colors combined
in exquisite brown, a conglomeration to represent
everything, a forty-thousand-year-old rock formation.
Your eyes.

Still the water in your hands runs clearer,
their angle being immensely more efficient.
In this world you made for me—where the colored sunrise
runoff smells of patchouli, where a great black sunflower
heart beats in my breakfast dish, and I have my fill of light
without ever having to swallow—the bird I was once
never rests, for her need, like that for wings,
is of a stronger beauty.

Love Poem

What the other animals already know: yes, the spring
still needs a soul. When you gave birth
into a basket of stars, they mutated.

A wave crashes over you in the future.
But how will you know violence as we have seen it?
Who will you hide, high in the mountains

in hopes she will prepare for your journey
of solitude with utmost deliberance?
The child weaned on mountain air expels prayers

like breaths. This hermitess will hold you in the folds
of her cloak-black stars sewn with beads of blacker dew.
But Great Stranger, where will you settle tonight?

In what cradle or child's bed will you sleep?
You could flaunt your great lineage of stars,
trailing forever in every direction, but your eternity

is no longer enough. Your omniscience is missing
depth, as though you yourself are an amnesiac.
If you remember who you are, then please:

strike the matches, and turn around three times.
Close your eyes and, in the void of white noise,
command the silence to begin again.

Love Poem

I begin by tracing circles on your back.
The darkness speaks to me as well.
So many traditions ask me to cover my eyes,
but you are my unicorn. You never ask me not to look.
Only in prayers have I heard you cry. The weeping stream,
the guardian of doves of sorrow. Only the pigeons flock
to your windows. What if I were a pigeon
in the naked space of your eternity? What if
I were alive?

In the dark the priest unlocks the door to the altar.
I promise, I love you. He counts the nights
until evil dwindles. Patience.

The certainty of the half-bird wanes. Fragmented
speech, fragmented abbeys. Alleys of finance,
semi-articulate. How heavy is the sleep of love?

Grandmother's Love Poem

Old shepherds wake to the change in the beat of the night—
dying heartbeats slow to flapping fish on the drumskin.
The sky yellowed at his, her edges, spotted with age, is stretched
leprously from the edges of the earth overhead. Grandmother
sings to us in a burning gold voice. It is hundreds of degrees
in the world, and we are too slow to drink, too slow
to think in words—we must rely on imagined blue space, on inches
of green so rare they redeem us—before we burst into the fire again.
We are burning under grandmother's quilt, knitted from the edges
of leaves, the seeing hands of ancient trees. She calls to us with sea
breezes, and we shiver with the repulse of desire; we want to be
loved with water, with all the shades of the blue we've been promised
in God's fairytales.

Love Poem

How can I promise anything other than to weep for you?
The questions you kept hidden have grown old; they've changed
in captivity, away from your eyes, from cocoons to moths
with no wings; brown, alone. You never thought to let them go;
instead you cradled the minute, deformed corpses as though
you were a new mother: patient, proud, helpless—
unconvincing. The lessons you learned long ago—how to be
a whole man not entirely a woman, how to detect a heartbeat
through thick snow—you might have taught these to your wingless
children. No half a heart, no half a night's snow, no other man
could be so tender. We wander through woods together, slowly,
balancing the sun above our chests. You walk in light as though
you had once worn a halo. You light up—a thorn has brushed
my thigh, and your lips turn red. You have never been quite
so somber as you profess, old friend.

Love Poem

Let this day be holy: it has yet to learn the language
of steel, for it hails from the gray sodden dialect
of rain: pouring, pouring, torrential. Together
we shine on, under the polished sky, until our little
bed of land is no longer nearby. This day cannot
be ruined. It must be sacred, as today I have decided
to name myself after the old woman of the Lake
and her skirt of depths, keeper of its magic: Lake Angela.
We skate over water's layers with little wonder
what holds up our breath. I named myself previously
after a glimmer that turned out to be the shadow
of a murderous death. I no longer know that person
clearly, though I care for her sorrows within the wells
of my memory. Sometimes I allow soft music to drift
in—when it is free of any threat of language
and does not pose the danger of setting these wells
to boil. I have a hard time letting this day rest, because
it is holy, and because it is the same as any day
for my soul, flapping at the feeble bars of the straw
cage, iron with principle. My soul, awkward as a fly,
is as honorable and small, large only with the potential
for a great, black-winged disease. How easily the cat
tires of his incessant preaching.

Love for the Sad Old One

My words to the sad old one leave him uneven;
he knows his due. The poems glide up their stems
into blooms noxious to him. The colors inherent
in the sky—dormant to most, powerful yet benign—
reveal themselves to him and drip pain into his eyes.
He will not eat a word held from my hand, only
my mouth, and now it is too late to feed him well
what once was spilling, was far too plenty.
In the dark in his eyes with the lights extinguished
where he planned to stay alone and to hide, strangers
come looking for us.

Saint's Love Poem

The weak corpse evokes enough light.
The holes in the eyes wake.
My burning life breaks like a wave.

In dark rooms it comes to life. An old sea
housing ancient fishes. With fear's red glow.

A saint stands in the green grotto before
her sainthood. She searches for her soul
in the blue wind, looking for her name
among the memories, rabbits, the lapis lazuli.

My rose has choked to death;
her black mouth surrounds my lips and sucks
out black breaths from my inner dark.

Lighten my earth, I murmur.
Add to my soul, she cries.

The Rules of the Dream

I.

Just as I am sure that the authorities of Science will come,
the town sloughs off its bricks, as land shaves off its cliffs,
the smoother and ever more perilous, to spit formal words out:
it is forbidden. I wish to give birth to birds and stars, beings so sharp.
I think the sky is very brave to lift them up, every morning to fight
a red war for feather or last twilit flicker. I want God
for my mother and my lover, something ancient to make its home
in me. I desire both the sharp and the helpless: things I can count on
never to be gray. Sometimes gold birds fly by on foreign streams
of rich laughter, ripping through God's gray cataracts that hang
over us as heavy clouds. Perfect pain, such beauty frightens me;
but I want to be the one to give birth to birds and stars and the words
that will kill us in the end.

II.

There is a winding stair submerged in Lake water
and a child, half drowned, our savior in red hair, red light.
From the mooning fortress stained dark, glass stars sink
slowly into the gaping mouths of fish—the boy has no
blood, but Lake in his pale veins—that pull the lighthouse
with its white armor onward. The clang of the ship's edges
strikes the dark. A mariner in the vacuum of night stands
erect on board the deck, where he wilts without sunlight
like clover, like the winged petals of bitter-yellow bees.

III.

I awoke at night wondering if the green light was meant
for me or for someone else. My veins ached like soft beds
of silt around hard needles, though I have never abused
my body in that way. Two years after one of me has died, I find
his last scream, open-mouthed but silent, in the shower—at last
—and the tears stream down my ankles, whirling drainward
with possibility. I weep for control of my mouth. Remember,
even if you love yourself you must marry someone else.

IV.

The rules of the dream evade me by morning, trick me
into waking up. Time smells like jasmine when the wind
just wants you to keep sleeping, chewing on dreams;
the cow savors the sound of the horn, with the Lake's lighthouse
removed and hidden high in the Alps. The music listens back
for echoes, emptying, the fine stone of my fingers worn away at last.
My one, it won't matter ever again how much I love you. I will wait
here pouring out snow until the blackbird whispers otherwise. Mean-
while, the heart hangs on ice. His death still disturbs me: I still can't see
through it. I plaster sandpaper to the walls in this apartment while I wait.
I rise each night at ten, warning your eyes of blackness, licking
your stars' black ice, scrolling your tongue like Torah. It is time
for me to dust off the moon, the birds' soot-laden nests. You realize
that if we had a child it would grow up and leave us as I did my parents.
I am always gestating words anyway, so if any self makes more
than sense, cradle her; kill the rest.

Fragments of Love Poems

Our souls came from the same bag—
like luminescent flowers excluded from sunlight,
translucent, sky-bearing seeds.
It is my special talent to suffer nostalgia for someplace
I cannot remember, something I have never seen.
I return home and the people there

no longer lament their lack of wings.

To all those I've never encountered, I miss you now. To all my friends
who are ghosts, you've never tried. In coiled wire, around a telephone
pole, the nests of fluff and sinew swing the black-eyed baby birds.

Where does your flute stone voice hail from, rivering?

I was led to the cave where the dark spoke to me as my native child.
"O see the spiderlight!"
I think it has forgotten me. Daytime
and the river burns with fever. It courses through town
with ragged edges where the young wash and sun.
They drape white clothes over jagged rock teeth, the grinding saw song
from the distance severed by churchyard chimes.
Even the weather stutters as God steps slowly across the stream,
tufts of fur and mange on her back.
She tells me, "Be happier than you can; happier than God
made you."
"I am tired all the time, and my mind is dull: I can cut nothing with it."
"Rest now. Find beauty in your sleep."

No more making love in darkness—more light!
Nightingale plays across piano keys.
The base of the mountain sings.
She smokes music. She laughs music.
The blue horses of my dreams—
skin spasms, bones of silk and jade.

Who is the master of sorrow? (I must, I must meet her.)
The end? The jackhammers applaud in my head.

I'm still in the yellow room, not yet quiet enough to name myself.
It was not allowed to be longer than this, my lover, my mother.
My breasts rise and fall as the breaths invade
and correct.
Love, there are children in the hours.
See, I love. Without light, even my night starves.

Love Poem

You are inconsolable.
Like an ocean
in your bucket, between the thyme
and the mint. You often freeze
beneath my image. I bend over you
and the stars go out—
lashes of wisteria, purple
ashes of heaven's remains.
You are inconsolable,
and I don't blame you.

Love Poem

Last night
    your screams
of blue
    woke me from a drowning sleep:
the sky was pouring time
    from steep edges,
hours torrential from the precipice,
    seconds sodden with anticipation,
the clocks on earth full of uncanny foreboding and perspiring.

Is this abundance not enough?

Perhaps your pious fear is warranted. Perhaps
with tomorrow or even today I will fly from here
on new yellow wings—gifted to me by the hours—
without you. Maybe your fear surprises you.

Maybe I will not fall.

The truth is you have nothing
to fear, not even the prison made of abundant
blooming lights and prayer, for you know:
how could I prepare for the night
without you?

Love Poem

I am the black spear that cuts
through black water.

I am the thriving shadow that sprawls
across your palm as it grows.

I am the small cry your mandible
utters every time you command
the bone to descend, then rise.

You don't know the sadness that begins
where you profess to end:
your footsteps stop sounding.

I have tasted myself, and I taste
of milk, of the milk of angels gone
silver, slender in trickles, a path
that leads to forever
                                forever to sadness.

I am the thorn in the pad of your foot.
I am the foot on which you stand.

I rejoice in the rainbow of fallen colors.
I renounce in painful anguish
all that stems from me.

I Return to Find Layers of Dust
Over the Dream

It is safe to tell you now: I have become friendly
with my Sickness. It has found a home in me, and even I
know how difficult finding a home can be. And I have adjusted:
as I perform the household chores, gracefully, carefully—unlike
before—I sing my Sickness its lullaby brimming with yokes
of children in green. This Sickness was lonely

before it belonged to me. We peel an onion together and cry.
The mutant in my vanity extends from many origins,
charming children's games. I hang on, on my knees before
the bridges of spring. A cold feather writes on the wind
in broad strokes I admire, loose strokes at ease as the sea
beneath my bedroom. Fear falls in the blood; it flowers.
A swamp inside me greens in the absence of a human voice,
a windblown soul, a seed.

The recurring dream of childhood feathers its blue lace over
my eyes like a web. The holiness I used to hold captive leaves
no marks. Without eyes, after all, the prophetess sees. Without
gods, the raging God roars upon death, without a bed
of its own, a cradle, or a nest. I may not be able to withstand
the turbulence of my hopes in you.

I was happy once in a corner of our earth I came to know
by heartbeats—ours coincided. What nonsense words convey.
What presence means, meaning infinitely so much more!

Love Poem

You come, shake the dust from my heart—
the wind picks up into the fire of the lily storm,
anchored in the hour, like a house, by yellow-orange blooms—
long hard, full from promises. Who hears us
but the gray pigeons, the groans beneath the graying
dusk. We sing to the tones in the chest, together;
we come into the world unasked, yet it means so much.
I speak to you and don't understand the words myself.
Strange signs draw us together. The fruits on the trees,
once sweet, are now in love. I lock the birds in my mouth
lest their familiar songs prolong my estrangement.
I see in your direction a path, a stranger one—
that welcomes me.

Your shadow becomes entangled in the blue lights
of evening. I am the child of two great fears.
The red deer of autumn disappears from the hunt
like a moonlight switching off. You strike me with a word
so magnificent I want to die and let yours be
my last breath. I want to rest in blue waters—beneath
them a mirror, sparkling with reasons no mind can
understand, but will go on reflecting. Lead a far-off ship to shore.

The bottomless container of night is romantic as its depths.
If you can meet me in the wilderness, we will wash our charred
lineages; we will scour the carbon from our faultless dark.
Perhaps we have seen God in this night already
and have not recognized her. If I throw off my face,
will you catch my heart? Before time flies off, shaking
its dust onto my organs blooming like petals in your presence.
And what if my heart should snap on its stem and my voice
suddenly die? It would free you
to live in the world I have made for you, my love.

Love Poem

The long life of the stone stretches on;
our hearts would have fermented in time.

Why people don't trust the voices in their minds,
I don't know. The autobiography of a poem
is enough.

You open up spaces with your eyes. Yes, we have fallen,
but from what? (And when?) As the free deer moves—silks—
so do the caverns of heaven, the waves notched with salt
sculptures, with sinuous rocks, with serpents hugging spheres.

It is always World without Word now. One lives and dies
in a matter of silence, the traces of his old mannerisms still
spasming across the face. Stone.

And where we enter a future filled with mirrors of dreams,
the deer sees memories of a clearer time to be.
The One Great Sadness is from the beginning, was never
passed. On the one hand, memory; on the other, breath.

Even on our wedding night we go back to the womb—
to breath. We count on our fingers and our toes
the trees left to sustain us. The dead are sealed beneath
the lid of sky and left—to remember and to take it in—
the blackness of lives set to night. And stone.

Acknowledgments

Bombay Gin: "When It Is Time"
Neon: "A Foreign Hotel," "Early Memory of Hearing Colors,
    Holding a Cockroach"
The Perch: "Jesus' Ribs"
Shady Side Review: "Stranded (A Love Poem)"

The poems "Careful Asymmetry," "Toward Sleep," "Purification,"
"A Vision," "Old Magic," "God Also Moans," "This Is the Eye of Time,"
"Summer Rain," "Grandma Sings the Last Song," "Surrender," and
"Points" appeared in the chapbook *Old Magic* (! Press, 2010).

About FutureCycle Press

FutureCycle Press is dedicated to publishing lasting English-language poetry books, chapbooks, and anthologies in both print-on-demand and Kindle ebook formats. Founded in 2007 by long-time independent editor/publishers and partners Diane Kistner and Robert S. King, the press incorporated as a nonprofit in 2012. A number of our editors are distinguished poets and writers in their own right, and we have been actively involved in the small press movement going back to the early seventies.

The FutureCycle Poetry Book Prize and honorarium is awarded annually for the best full-length volume of poetry we publish in a calendar year. Introduced in 2013, our Good Works projects are anthologies devoted to issues of universal significance, with all proceeds donated to a related worthy cause. Our Selected Poems series highlights contemporary poets with a substantial body of work to their credit; with this series we strive to resurrect work that has had limited distribution and is now out of print.

We are dedicated to giving all of the authors we publish the care their work deserves, making our catalog of titles the most diverse and distinguished it can be, and paying forward any earnings to fund more great books.

We've learned a few things about independent publishing over the years. We've also evolved a unique, resilient publishing model that allows us to focus mainly on vetting and preserving for posterity poetry collections of exceptional quality without becoming overwhelmed with bookkeeping and mailing, fundraising activities, or taxing editorial and production "bubbles." To find out more about what we are doing, come see us at www.futurecycle.org.

The FutureCycle Poetry Book Prize

All full-length volumes of poetry published by FutureCycle Press in a given calendar year are considered for the annual FutureCycle Poetry Book Prize. This allows us to consider each submission on its own merits, outside of the context of a contest. Too, the judges see the finished book, which will have benefitted from the beautiful book design and strong editorial gloss we are famous for.

The book ranked the best in judging is announced as the prize-winner in the subsequent year. There is no fixed monetary award; instead, the winning poet receives an honorarium of 20% of the total net royalties from all poetry books and chapbooks the press sold online in the year the winning book was published. The winner is also accorded the honor of being on the panel of judges for the next year's competition; all judges receive copies of all contending books to keep for their personal library.

www.ingramcontent.com/pod-product-compliance
Lightning Source LLC
Chambersburg PA
CBHW070005100426
42741CB00012B/3118